Bless Your Heart:

Low-sodium Recipes for a Heart-healthy Lifestyle

by Tristi Pinkston

Other Titles by Tristi Pinkston:

Nothing to Regret
Strength to Endure
Season of Sacrifice
Agent in Old Lace
Secret Sisters
Dearly Departed
Hang 'em High

This book is not intended to diagnose or treat any disease, and the statements herein have not been evaluated by the American Medical Association. You are encouraged, as with any change in diet or exercise, to consult your primary care physician.

This cookbook has been formatted with an extra-deep margin so you can have it spiral bound, if you like. Just take it in to your local copy shop and they can do it for you.

ISBN-13: 978-1463634957

ISBN-10: 1463634951

Praise for Bless Your Heart

"I always thought low-sodium cooking was something I'd only do if a doctor insisted. Tristi has changed my mind. Her recipes are full of flavor and the salt is never missed. The whole family enjoyed them and best of all, they were easy to put together. After trying these, I'm much more excited to incorporate low-sodium recipes into my family's diet."
- Stephanie Humphreys, author of *Finding Rose* and *Double Deceit*

"Tristi's collection of recipes proves low sodium does not have to mean bland. I absolutely loved the carrot cake, and the other dishes I've tried are really tasty too!"
- Heather Justesen, author of *Blank Slate* and others

"I highly recommend *Bless Your Heart* for your family. My kids have absolutely loved each recipe we've tried. And as their mother, I feel good knowing they're eating delicious, nutritious meals."
- Danyelle Ferguson, author of *(dis)Abilities and the Gospel*

"Although my husband and I don't currently struggle with any particular low-sodium needs, we really enjoy the recipes Tristi let us try out from her new cookbook. My husband had no clue that dinner was low in sodium until I told him afterward—the other flavors in the dish kicked in nicely and there was no need to add anything else. The stuffed potatoes have become part of our 'must have again' list!"
- Paulette Inman

INTRODUCTION

Two years ago, my ear, nose, and throat specialist put me on a low-sodium diet in the belief that I might have Meniere's Disease. This condition is caused by too much water volume in the ear and results in hearing loss. By reducing the sodium in my diet, my doctor felt the water volume would decrease[1] and solve the mystery of the chronic ear problems I've had since I was a teenager.

I lived the diet faithfully for a month until it was time for my check-up. After carefully reviewing my charts and examining me, my doctor determined I did not have Meniere's Disease after all, and told me I could go off the low-sodium diet. I told him no.

Being on that diet cleared up many other physical conditions I've been struggling with and gave me answers I've been looking for. In the course of just one month:

1. My near-constant headaches subsided in frequency and severity.
2. I no longer woke up nauseated.
3. My periods became significantly lighter.
4. My bones and joints no longer hurt like they had in the past.
5. My fingers and ankles were no longer puffy.

When my doctor first put me on the diet, he told me I was going to hate him for it. But after living the diet for a month and seeing the remarkable changes it made in my life, I thanked him and told him it was the best thing he could have done for me.

---

[1] http://www.nidcd.nih.gov/health/balance/meniere.asp

The problem with my ears wasn't related to fluid retention at all, but in a way, I'm grateful for the experience. It led my doctor to suggest the low-sodium diet. Restricting salt intake is usually recommended for patients who have high blood pressure, and I've never had a blood pressure problem. In fact, my numbers are generally on the low side. Yet, going low sodium turned out to be the answer to the above-listed health conditions when nothing else worked. I never thought I'd be grateful for my ear problems, but they opened a path toward a proper course of treatment.

Is This Book for You?

If you're seeing yourself in my story, you may experience significant relief in living the low-sodium diet, as I have. There's certainly no harm in giving it a try. However, as we all have different systems and different metabolisms, your results will be unique. I only know what has worked for me.

You may want to conduct a month-long experiment to see if this diet is a solution for you. You may find that your symptoms go away and you might find that other health concerns are suddenly better. Any attempt made to lower sodium can only be a good thing.

Check with your doctor for his recommendations. If he has already suggested that you live a low-sodium diet, he may have given you a sodium range that would be most beneficial to you. My specialist asked me to remain between 400-1000 mg. of sodium per day, and this amount was verified by the Web sites I visited about Meniere's Disease.[2] I feel best when I remain around 1000 mg. Again, our bodies are all different, and what's right for me might not be right for you. If your doctor gives you a generous leeway of 2000

---

[2] http://oto2.wustl.edu/men/sodium.htm

mg., this is still lower than the national average of 6000 mg. per day.[3] If you feel this intake is still a little high, you can take it down a bit, but ask your doctor if there are any health reasons that might keep you from wanting to try for 400-1000 mg.

Regardless of the range you've been given for your own situation, the recipes in this book will be beneficial to you. Each has been created with the lowest sodium content possible for that type of item. You'll find great flexibility as you mix and match, and add modified versions of your own favorite recipes, as well.

What Does It Mean to Go on a Low-Sodium Diet?

It takes a huge amount of willpower to turn away from those salty foods we all love and embark on a low-sodium diet. It means that fast food is a thing of the past. Processed meats, like ham and bologna, are gone. No longer will we munch down a pickle (those things are processed in salt brine, you know). We will eschew the pizza. We will stand up and walk away in the face of potato chips. We will sit at the dinner table stolidly, chewing our salads, and feeling self-righteous at our strength and integrity.

Right? Isn't that what we have to do?

Yes and no.

We do need to exercise willpower. We do need to make fast food a rare occurrence, and pickles aren't such a great idea. But we can learn to do all these things in moderation. We can still have a slice of pizza from time to time, when balanced out with low-sodium meals the rest of the day. We can eat food that actually tastes like food and that fills us

[3] http://www.fda.gov/fdac/foodlabel/sodium.html

up—there's no starvation involved here. It might seem like it, because so many of our favorite foods are through-the-roof full of sodium, but there is life with less salt, and that's what we're here today to discuss.

Going low sodium means taking a little more time to read labels at the store. It means making several small decisions that add up to create one huge improvement in our health. It means cooking from scratch more often and paying closer attention to what we eat. But it doesn't mean shutting ourselves away in a hut in the middle of the woods and refusing to enjoy life.

But I Don't Put a Lot of Salt on My Food

After doing some research and learning more about sodium and its affect on health in general and my health in particular, I was excited. I just had to tell everyone what I learned. What surprised me was that every single person said, "But I don't put a lot of salt on my food." That is the first major misconception people have about sodium. In their minds, sodium equals salt, salt comes from a shaker, and if they don't shake salt on their food, they're eating a low-sodium diet. That's just simply not true. Many foods contain a great deal of sodium naturally.

We would never sprinkle salt on our pizza, but a slice of pepperoni pizza has 770 mg. of sodium. That fact probably didn't shock you, but let me go on. Take cottage cheese, the classic diet food. One serving of cottage cheese contains around 440 mg of sodium. That's straight out of the carton, without adding anything to it. One slice of bread has over 100 mg, and one tortilla has 300 mg. One ounce of cheddar cheese has 180 mg, and light ranch dressing has 390 mg. in two tablespoons. That's just an example of the way you ingest far more salt than you realize without ever reaching for the shaker.

Visit **www.calorieking.com** for an excellent search engine to look up sodium content in all your favorite foods.

So, Why is Salt Bad for Me?

The most common reason to cut back the amount of salt in your diet is to reduce the symptoms of hypertension, also known as high blood pressure.[4] Hypertension can lead to heart attacks and heart disease, which is the #1 killer of both men and women.[5] Of course, hypertension is not the sole cause of heart disease. There are other causes, such as high cholesterol, and we are encouraged to find a diet that contains less than 300 mg. of cholesterol per day[6] for optimum heart health. Incidentally, many of the recipes in this book are also low in cholesterol, although that is not the main focus.

Hypertension can be caused by an abnormality of the heart, inflexibility of the arteries, obesity, age, and genetics. It's also caused by over-consumption of sodium.[7] When we eat too much sodium, we overload our kidneys, whose job it is to remove the excess sodium from our bodies, and they can develop renal insufficiency and failure.[8]

---

[4] http://www.fda.gov/fdac/foodlabel/sodium.html

[5] http://www.americanheart.org/presenter.jhtml?identifier=4478

[6] http://www.americanheart.org/presenter.jhtml?identifier=1510

[7] http://www.medicinenet.com/high_blood_pressure/page4.htm

[8] Ibid.

Other conditions make it difficult for our bodies to use sodium, including liver and lung diseases. If you have liver, lung, heart, or kidney disease, you will want to check with your doctor about your sodium intake.

Sodium can cause our tissues to swell, making it harder for our hearts to pump to the affected areas. High blood pressure leads to heart attacks, strokes, and aneurysms, which occur when blood bursts through vessels weakened by high blood pressure.[9] High blood pressure influences many other organs and systems throughout the body.

Also keep in mind that high sodium can lead to left ventricular hypertrophy, a condition which enlarges your heart's main pumping chamber and lessens its ability to function properly.[10] Considering how crucial heart health is to our very existence, we need to pay immediate attention to the factors that will lead to increased heart health. We should become educated and we should take action.

Don't Eliminate Salt Completely

You might be thinking, "Well, if less salt is good, I'll go no salt and it will be even better." Right? Wrong. Salt is a necessary mineral. We must consume a certain amount of it in order to remain healthy—at least 400 mg daily, with some experts suggesting 500 mg. daily.[11] Salt maintains our electrolyte balance. It keeps the fluid ratio in our bodies stabilized. It prevents hypothermia—in fact, wilderness hikers are known to carry salt tablets with them in their backpacks.

---

[9] http://www.mayoclinic.com/health/high-blood-pressure/HI00062

[10] Ibid.

[11] http://www.feinberg.northwestern.edu/nutrition/factsheets/sodium.html

When we exercise, we must replace the salt lost through sweating. This is why athletes will sometimes drink Gatorade or other sports drinks which contain sodium as well as electrolytes. Gatorade has 110 mg. of sodium per 8 oz. serving, which isn't a lot, but enough to help regain that fluid balance in the body.

Expectant mothers should also be careful not to let their salt levels go too low. They need to keep their fluids in balance, especially amniotic fluids. On the other hand, too much salt will result in the swelling of hands, feet, and internal tissues which leads to preeclampsia,[12] a potentially fatal condition. Swelling isn't just limited to pregnant women, though. We can all suffer from water retention—male and female, pregnant or not. Sometimes it's just annoying and makes us feel fat, but other times it signals an underlying medical condition and we should seek our doctor's opinion.

Not everyone will find their blood pressure decreasing as they eliminate salt. This has led some experts to think that limiting salt consumption isn't as important as the current studies would have us believe.[13] It's true that for some, blood pressure won't change dramatically. Yet blood pressure isn't the only way to tell if you should lower your sodium intake. My blood pressure has always been perfectly normal, and yet I'm experiencing much better overall health as a result of the low-sodium diet.

An Adjustment Phase

When you first start eating low-sodium dishes, your first inclination will be to reach for the salt shaker. We are so accustomed to eating salty foods that it's hard to eat

---

[12] http://www.aafp.org/afp/20041215/2317.html

something we perceive as bland. Resist the urge to add salt to your dish. It will only make the adjustment take that much longer.

My first day on the low-sodium diet, I felt picked on. I wondered why the cosmos was choosing to punish me in such a particularly brutal way. It was unfair! But by the second day, and yes, it really was that fast, I could tell a difference in the way my body felt. I wasn't achy. My headache was gone. And by the end of that week, I knew this principle was one I should live permanently.

I can't guarantee you'll stop feeling picked on after just one day. It may take longer for you. Your body does have an adjustment to make. You will experience a slight drop in blood volume as the sodium, which was inflating that volume, is no longer wreaking havoc on your system. You will probably crave salt, which isn't a bad thing—we do need some salt in our bodies to stay healthy, and a craving is your body's way of reminding you to take care of it. Just don't go overboard.

In addition, the recipes in this book really are delicious! You won't feel like you're "settling" or "making do." You will feel satisfied and you will be full. Just check out the sample menu on page 132 if you don't believe me—there's a lot of food on that list.

After a few days, you'll find that your desire to reach for the salt shaker has diminished. You'll appreciate the wide variety of flavors in your food and you'll have a sense of well-being that you're doing something healthy for your heart and for your life. I strongly encourage you to hang in there until you've reached that point. Your health, and your heart, will thank you for it.

---

[13] http://www.realage.com/nutritioncenter/articles.aspx?aid=10383

But What about Special Occasions?

It's your anniversary and your sweetie wants to take you to dinner at that new restaurant everyone loves. You can go, and you can enjoy yourself—but I highly recommend that your meal choices earlier in the day and for a few days afterward be low in sodium to help reestablish the proper saline balance in your body.

You can enjoy a handful of potato chips, you can eat some pretzels—you don't have to cut out salty food entirely, as long as you keep it in balance. One single-serving bag of Lay's Original potato chips has 180 mg. If you pair that with a low-sodium sandwich, you haven't blown anything.

There is a danger, however—salt is addictive. We eat a little and we want a little more. In fact, Lay's even admits it with their slogan, "No one can eat just one." It's not just the potato chip—it's the salt that goes with it. So if you go out to dinner with your spouse tonight, and to lunch with a friend tomorrow, and you swing by a drive-through window the day after that, your body is going to get reprogrammed to eating high quantities of salt, and you'll have to go through the whole adjustment process again, not to mention the spikes in your blood pressure from the increase of sodium. Go out from time to time, but balance it with proper eating habits.

Most chain restaurants have Web sites you can visit to view a nutrition guide which will tell you the sodium contents of the dishes they serve. These charts are frequently posted on the wall at the restaurant itself. If you have a question about a dish, don't hesitate to ask the server. Even if they don't have a Web site or a chart on the wall, as might be the case with a higher-end restaurant or a locally-owned establishment, they probably have a booklet outlining their menu. If you're at a higher-end restaurant, you can always ask to speak to the chef. Keep in mind that some of the sauces, etc, might be made in large batches and there may be little the chef can do to lower the sodium in an individual dish, but he might be able to recommend a meal that doesn't have a high sodium content to begin with.

When eating fast food, be careful—the salads available at most fast food establishments actually have more sodium than the sandwiches, by the time you add on the toppings. I recommend you avoid fast food as much as possible, but at times when it's either eat now or faint, choose your meal carefully. See page 140 for recommendations at some of your favorite fast food restaurants.

I know if I'm not selective, I can feel the increase in blood pressure in my chest by the tightening of muscles around my heart, and I feel the pressure building in the back of my head, leading to a headache. You might be able to tell when you've had too much sodium at one meal too. These physical sensations are warning signs to tell us we've done damage to ourselves. The trick is to remain within our safe perimeter so we don't have to experience those uncomfortable warnings.

But I Like Salt!

I think it's safe to say we all like salt. Come on—who doesn't crave potato chips, French fries, pizza, and pretzels? Who doesn't like the way salt perks up the other flavors in our meal? As we've discussed, sodium is something our bodies need, but as we practice eating it in moderation, we'll discover something—there's a whole world out there, filled with other flavors.

The tang of citrus, the pungent zap of ginger and curry, the liveliness of chili powder—not everything has to taste like salt. When we retrain our palates to appreciate these other flavors, we might even find that salty tastes aren't as appealing to us anymore. Certainly, these other flavors are more subtle than salt, and we need to tap into them in order to really savor them, but that's part of the fun of eating—to concentrate on the dish and enjoy all the layers of taste and texture.

What about Weight Loss?

Going on a low-sodium diet does not automatically mean you're going to lose weight. You will find a reduction of water weight, but the fat cells aren't affected so easily. You will still need to burn those off.

I do also encourage you to read labels. When a product advertises itself as being low fat, they've usually bumped up the sodium to make the food taste better. It works the other way, too—when you buy something labeled low sodium, you may find a higher fat content.

Your best food tool for weight loss is found in the produce section. Filling your stomach with good, fresh produce, moderated with lean meats, dairy products, and quality grains will encourage your system to lose weight naturally. It's also fun to realize that many of these foods are naturally low sodium. You can live a low-sodium diet and lose weight at the same time, but primarily if you make the conscious effort to do so. Eating a bag of low-sodium candy every day, for instance, will not help your weight-loss efforts, even though the candy has less sodium than your usual choice.

Not every low-sodium cookbook on the market is a weight-loss cookbook. However, in this volume, you'll find that many of the recipes are low in fat and full of protein, as well as having low salt content.

When I first began this lifestyle, I immediately lost two pounds of water weight. However, my weight problems stem mostly from other causes: not enough exercise, low thyroid function, and a sugar addiction. While the low sodium diet has helped my overall health tremendously, I still need to work on these other areas in order to completely overcome my weight problems.

Learning to Comparison Shop

When you're grocery shopping, be sure to compare the labels on the different brands of food. Not every manufacturer uses the same recipe, and sodium levels will vary a great deal as you compare. For instance, a can of Del Monte tomatoes with Italian seasoning contains 520 mg. per serving. The store brand of the exact same product has 330 mg. per serving. That's quite a difference. However, by being willing to substitute, we can work some magic. The store brand of chopped tomatoes, no salt added, has only 20 mg. per serving. If you get that and add your own oregano and basil, you've saved yourself 500 mg. over Del Monte, and the taste difference is practically unnoticeable.

I used to buy one certain brand of flour tortilla, and then I checked the label. 400 mg. for one little tortilla—wow! I checked the content on the other brands on the store shelf. I found one for 300 mg. Not bad, but still a little high. With a bit of searching, I found a package for 249 mg. It's still not low, but I can work that into my diet with some compromise, and I even like the taste better than I did my original brand.

So the next time you're at the grocery store, don't just grab whatever package is closest at hand, or even the one that's on sale. Read the sodium content. I've been amazed at how much sodium I was able to cut out of my diet just by getting Brand B over Brand A.

But Isn't It Expensive to Go Low Sodium?

At times, it seems like there's a conspiracy. Organic food is more expensive than non-organic. Whole grains are more expensive than white flour. Free-range chicken is always more pricey. If you're living on a budget, you seem forced to eat the high-calorie, low-nutrition foods that are made available to us.

It's true that buying low-sodium food is a little more expensive, in some ways. For instance, a can of green beans will sell for around fifty cents. A can of no-salt-added beans will sell for just under a dollar, depending on where you shop. That's twice the expense, right there.

But look at it another way. When you go low sodium, you will automatically stop ordering pizza or going by the drive through as often. You'll be cooking more from scratch, which is almost always less expensive. If you keep an eye on your produce and consume it before it spoils, there will be less fridge waste. Overall, your food budget will go down, even though the occasional item will cost a little bit more.

But What about the Kids?

I wish I could tell you my kids have been happy guinea pigs throughout my transition to a low-sodium lifestyle. I have one son who would live entirely on Lucky Charms and watermelon if I let him, and feeding him *anything* is hard. He's been my most difficult sell. My other children have gone along a little more willingly, but let's face it—today's kids would rather have a Happy Meal® than almost anything else. Making a healthy dinner and expecting everyone at the table to like it is a little bit unrealistic.

However, let me say this. If we can get our children to understand the necessity of eating healthy now, while they're young and adaptable, we will be saving them countless health problems down the road. If they understand the need to use moderation in their eating habits, to balance their meals and activities in ways that allow them to live at their healthiest, we could help them extend their lives by years.

I don't believe in completely restricting treats. All that does is make the child more eager to eat them when they are available. I see nothing wrong with occasional desserts and occasional meals out. When these are included in a healthy lifestyle and balanced with plenty of fruits, vegetables, and proteins, they are just fine. But when they are the norm, we are setting our children up for health problems as adults.

Your children may squawk and bellyache. I say, let them. If you're going to live a low-sodium diet for yourself, and yet continue to feed your children a high-sodium diet, you're not doing them any favors. You should feed your children the same way you're feeding yourself. It's good for their health, it's good for their character, and it will save you from making two meals instead of just one.

Their palates will eventually adjust. We discussed going through an adjustment phase—your children will go through it too. The benefits will far outweigh the squawking. My seven-year-old stopped complaining of pain in his legs shortly after we began the diet, pain I had attributed to growing pains that I too had at his age. But then I realized I was experiencing less pain in my limbs as well. It was connected, and now it's gone.

As with most kinds of tough love, your children will eventually thank you for it. "Maybe not today, and maybe not tomorrow, but soon, and for the rest of your life!"

But It's So Inconvenient

My biggest problem with going low sodium was the fact that very few prepared foods are low salt. I'm a mom with four children. I homeschool. I'm a media reviewer, an editor, and an author. I have a church calling. I'm a busy person, and I often skip meals altogether. When I do eat, I tend to reach for something already made that I can warm up or even just open and eat. I do make more of an effort with dinner, but the rest of the time, it's sandwiches for the kids' lunch and maybe one for me too, if I remember.

When I realized I had to go on a low-sodium diet, I went into a bit of a tailspin. What would I eat? I would have to drop everything three times a day and create a meal from scratch. My precious time would have to be spent in the kitchen, and that meant less time at all my other tasks, and I was feeling harried before. How could I make this new lifestyle work with my already-established routines?

To be honest, I couldn't. I had to make some changes, and I freaked myself out a little bit at first. After I got done freaking out, I made some modifications, and I realized—it wasn't as bad as I'd made it out to be. I could do it. There were ways.

First, on days when I had a little more time, I could make double or even triple the batch of dinner, and freeze the other portions. I learned that a saucy recipe does better in one of those plastic dishes that go from the freezer to the microwave to the dishwasher—if you put a saucy dish in a freezer bag, half the sauce sticks to the inside of the bag and it's hard to get it all out. I can't tell you what a relief it is to know I have eight or ten dinners in my freezer, ready to pull out at a moment's notice.

I also like taking leftovers and putting them in smaller containers in the freezer. These become my lunches. If the kids are having peanut butter and I want to save my sodium budget for dinner, I'll grab one of those smaller containers out of the freezer and zap it. Poof—instant low-sodium lunch.

Another thing I learned is that low-sodium recipes don't have to take any longer to prepare than "usual" recipes. In fact, all the recipes in this book are remarkably easy. I wouldn't have even tried them myself if they weren't!

I also discovered I can prepare dinner during lunchtime. If things are a little quiet while I'm making lunch, I can get dinner ready and put it in the fridge, and then warm it at dinnertime. Or, I can do whatever chopping is called for and put those ingredients in the fridge until later. Use the time you have when you have it, and don't worry if you don't have all kinds of time at five o'clock every evening. Who does?

Every so often, when I have a slow day, I like to mix up several batches of low-sodium cookies or breakfast muffins and put those in the freezer as well. They're on hand all the time so if we get snacky (which is a lot) we have a low-sodium alternative.

You'll notice I mention freezers quite often in this book. I'm a firm believer in a large stand-up or chest freezer. If you have one, I encourage you to start using it to hold foods you can heat up in a flash. If you don't have one, I encourage you to get one. Sometimes you can find them on sale in the newspaper, but even if you end up buying new from the store, you will discover they are worth every penny. Several of my friends prepare meals for an entire month and freeze them, and only end up cooking one day in every thirty. How awesome is that? I've never made an entire month's worth, but even having a week's worth is a weight off my shoulders, freeing up my time and making it easier for me to access the low-sodium meals I need to keep in balance.

As you forge ahead with your new goals, you'll find your own ways to make it easier on yourself. The important thing is that you keep trying, and that you don't give up just because it's a little bit inconvenient sometimes. With advance planning, you can make it work for you.

How Do I Use This Cookbook?

I have only included recipes that are 400 mg. of sodium per serving or less. This allows you to have breakfast, lunch, and dinner without going over your sodium budget as you decide what to eat each day. For instance, if you'd really like to eat the Chicken and Mushrooms in Parmesan Cream Sauce for dinner, and you know it comes in at 273 mg., you can eat a 400 mg. lunch and still have 200 mg. for breakfast, and remain perfectly within your target range. I do encourage you to think about your meals a little bit in advance, not only so you can thaw whatever meat you might be using, but so you can plan how to spread out your sodium. If you know you're going to lunch with a friend, you can eat the Apple Raisin Oatmeal for breakfast, which has no sodium, and save yourself some salt that way.

Sit down and go through the book, noting which recipes sound the tastiest to you. As you try them, keep track of your favorites—I've included a wide variety and I'm sure there are foods here that will appeal to everyone. Then, as you plan your menu, just be sure to take note of the sodium content. I wouldn't recommend putting three meals of 400 mg. each all in one day, just as I wouldn't recommend putting three meals of 70 mg. all in one day. Keep in mind—your body does need at least 400 mg. for proper function, and as salt is water soluble, it washes out of your body and you have to renew it. Three meals of 70 mg. each in one day will only provide 210 mg., leaving your body lacking.

If you get to the end of your day and discover you've used up your sodium budget and still need a side dish for dinner, don't give up and reach for the macaroni and cheese. A green salad, chock full of vegetables, will be just the ticket. If you use extra tomatoes, they will provide the moisture the salad needs without raising the sodium content, or you could use a dribble of the blue cheese or ranch dressings found in the book. See the sample menu in the back for ideas on how to balance your sodium intake throughout the day.

The key to successfully living a low-sodium diet is learning how to substitute. While making your favorite recipes, use alternatives for the usual ingredients. Most of the time, the taste difference will only be a little noticeable, and you may even grow to enjoy the low-sodium version better.

There are two major substitutions I want to encourage you to make right now. These changes will save you countless grams of sodium throughout the course of a day.

First, choose unsalted butter over regular butter or margarine. One teaspoon of butter has 39 mg. and margarine has around 40 mg., depending on the brand. Unsalted butter has none. Some might say, "But butter has fat in it!" Yes, it does contain fat. But if you're not eating fast food, you've cut the fat intake in your diet, and you can afford to reintroduce some. Besides, your body needs a little bit of fat. It helps your brain work and it keeps your skin from drying out.

Second, get some sodium-free baking powder. I buy mine at my local health food store. It's made by Hain Pure Foods and I pay around $5.00 for an 8 oz. can, which is a little pricey when compared to the regular stuff. However, this product will allow you to enjoy cakes and cookies, recipes for which are found in this book. In addition, this powder contains no aluminum, unlike many of the other brands of baking powder on the market.

These are the two main substitutions I encourage. Others are to use unsalted canned vegetables instead of salted, look for low-sodium canned soups and broths, and to cook from scratch as much as possible.

You can take these principles and apply them to your own recipes as well. If you've got a dish you just love, you can go through it and modify it to have less sodium. You can take out the salt or cut it in half. You can dice up tomatoes and onions to use in place of salsa. You can use a reduced-sodium cream soup. You can use half the cheese. As you read through your recipes, I'm sure you'll think of ways you can reduce the sodium content in your favorite dishes. They might not taste exactly the same, but they'll be much healthier for you.

A quick note about portion sizes—we've become accustomed to eating more meat than we really need for optimum health. The meat portions in this book are based on a 4 oz. per serving scale, or roughly half a chicken breast. By eating a little less meat and concentrating instead on the vegetables and other accents, we'll not only lower our sodium intake naturally, but improve our cholesterol as well.

This dietary change may be one of the most important things you will ever do for your health, and you can and should be excited about it. Have some fun! Experiment! Going low sodium really isn't a death sentence—it's a new lease on life.

"All the knowledge I possess everyone else can acquire,

but my heart is all my own."

Johann Wolfgang von Goethe

Recipes

"Optimism is a kind of heart stimulant - the digitalis of failure."

Elbert Hubbard

Breakfast

It's no lie—breakfast is the most important meal of the day. It sets the tone for everything else you do. If you grab a breakfast sandwich on your way to work, you've just blown your entire day's sodium budget in one fell swoop. Think about these healthy alternatives instead. Many of them can be made and frozen to pull out and enjoy as needed.

Breakfast Smoothie

(Serves one-200 mg. per serving)

1 c. milk

1 scoop vanilla protein powder

½ c. orange juice

½ banana

Place all the ingredients in your blender, and blend for thirty seconds. The protein powder will keep you going until you're able to grab a real meal.

Fruit Salad

(Serves six—24 mg. per serving)

6 c. mixed fruit, chopped

Suggestions: bananas, apples, pears, mandarin oranges, grapes, kiwi, watermelon, cantaloupe, strawberries, raspberries, pineapple

1 8 oz. yogurt, any flavor

Mix the fruit together in a large bowl and blend the yogurt throughout.

A tasty way to start the day, and your children will love this salad too!

Pancake Syrup

(0 mg.)

Mrs. Butterworth's Light syrup has 130 mg. of sodium in a three- tablespoon serving, which seems a little skimpy to me, especially if you're eating a short stack. This recipe will let you eat as much syrup as you want.

2 c. white sugar

1 c. water

Bring water and sugar to a boil, stirring constantly. Maintain the boil for two minutes, then remove from heat. Add:

1 t. vanilla

1 t. Mapeline flavoring

Stir together. Serve immediately, or allow to cool. The syrup will thicken as it cools, or for thicker syrup from the start, increase to three cups of sugar. Keep leftovers in the fridge to use another day—if there are any leftovers.

Pancakes

(Makes six pancakes—42 mg. per pancake)

1 ¼ c. flour

2 T. sugar

2 t. sodium-free baking powder

3 T. vegetable oil

1 1/3 c. milk

1 egg

Blend the dry ingredients, then add the wet ingredients and mix with a fork until just moistened. Pour onto a hot griddle or skillet and cook about two minutes on each side, until golden. Serve with pancake syrup (recipe on previous page).

Cranberry Sauce Muffins

(Makes 12 muffins—12 mg. per muffin)

1 ½ c. flour

½ c. sugar

2 t. sodium-free baking powder

½ t. cinnamon

½ t. ginger

½ c. unsalted butter

1 egg

½ c. cranberry sauce, whole berry

½ c. orange juice

In a large mixing bowl, stir together the dry ingredients. Cut in the butter with a fork or your fingers until the mixture resembles crumbs.

Combine the egg, cranberry sauce, and juice, then add to the dry ingredients and stir until just mixed. Spoon into paper-lined muffin tins. Bake at 400° for 19 to 20 minutes.

Raisin Bread

(Makes twelve slices—3 mg. per slice)

1 ¼ c. water

2 T. unsalted butter, room temperature

3 ¼ c. flour (bread flour if using a machine, all-purpose if mixing by hand)

¼ c. sugar

1 ½ t. yeast

2 t. cinnamon

¾ c. raisins

For bread machine: Place all ingredients in the pan of your machine, with the exception of the raisins. Add the raisins after the first kneading. Set for the "sweet bread" or "white bread" cycle.

For hand-mixing: Place the water in a large bowl, making sure it's warm, but not hot. Add the yeast and allow it to work for five minutes. Add the butter, sugar, cinnamon, and flour, and knead well. Add the raisins, then allow to rise for half an hour. Punch down and shape into loaf. Allow to rise another half hour until doubled in size, then bake at 350° until golden, roughly 35 minutes, but the time will vary based on your individual oven.

Carrot Pineapple Muffins

(Makes twelve muffins—11 mg. sodium per muffin)

1 ½ c. flour

2 t. sodium-free baking powder

½ c. vegetable oil

1 c. carrots, finely grated

½ c. sugar

1 t. vanilla

1 t. cinnamon

2 eggs, beaten well

½ c. crushed pineapple with juice

Preheat oven to 375° and place paper liners in muffin tin. Mix all ingredients together with a heavy-duty spoon—do not beat. Divide evenly into muffin cups. Bake for 25 minutes.

Almond Poppy Seed Bread

(Makes two loaves, twelve slices each—18 mg. per slice)

3 c. flour

2 c. sugar

1 ½ t. sodium-free baking powder

3 eggs

1 ½ c. milk

1 c. vegetable oil

1 t. vanilla extract

2 t. almond extract

2 T. poppy seeds

Mix all ingredients together with an electric beater for two minutes. Bake in two greased loaf pans at 350° for 55 minutes. If you don't happen to have poppy seeds, that's okay—the bread still tastes great.

Crab Quiche

(Serves four—213 mg. per serving)

¼ c. red bell pepper, chopped

2 T. onion, chopped

1 t. olive oil

4 oz. imitation crab

1 c. whole milk

2 eggs

3 T. nonfat dry milk powder

1/8 t. pepper

dash of nutmeg

2 oz. Swiss cheese, shredded

4 slices of tomato

Spray pie plate with nonstick cooking spray and preheat oven to 350°. In a skillet, combine oil, bell pepper, and onion, stir to coat, and sauté until tender crisp. Add crab and mix, then sprinkle in bottom of pie plate.

Whisk the milk, eggs, milk powder, pepper, and nutmeg, then add half the cheese. Pour mixture over the vegetables and crab. Place in hot oven and bake for 20 to 30 minutes, depending on your oven, until fully set and golden brown. Sprinkle remaining cheese on top and arrange tomatoes, then return to oven for 1 minute until cheese is melted. Let stand for 5 minutes.

Veggie Breakfast Bake

(Serves twelve—256 mg. per serving)

2 T. unsalted butter

2 medium leeks, (white parts only) quartered and sliced

6 asparagus spears, trimmed and diced

5 c. frozen southern-style hash browns

4 oz. pimientos, drained

½ t. dried dill

2 c. milk

1 c. Kraft Parmesan cheese

4 eggs

Preheat oven to 350°. Coat a 9x13 pan with nonstick spray. Melt butter in a skillet and sauté asparagus and leeks until tender crisp. Add the potatoes, pimientos, and dill, then toss lightly. Place evenly into the 9x13 pan.

Beat the eggs and milk together in a bowl. Add half the cheese, then pour over the potato mixture. Sprinkle with the rest of the cheese and cover pan with tin foil, baking for 45 minutes covered. Remove the foil and cook an additional 20 minutes, uncovered. Let stand for 15 minutes before serving.

This recipe will keep in the fridge for a couple of days, but does not freeze well.

Banana Pecan Cream of Wheat

(Serves six—56 mg. per serving)

4 c. water

¾ c. Cream of Wheat or other brand of farina

3 bananas, sliced

3 T. (heaping) brown sugar

2 oz. pecans, chopped

Bring water to boil in a saucepan, then add the Cream of Wheat. Stir until blended, then add the bananas, sugar, and pecans. Take off heat and allow to thicken slightly. Serve.

The trick is not to overcook. You want the cereal to be slightly runny when you take it off the heat. If you wait until it's thick, it will create glue in the bowl and then no one will want to eat it!

Cinnamon Applesauce Cream of Wheat

(Serves six—56 mg. per serving)

4 c. water

¾ c. Cream of Wheat or other brand of farina

½ c. raisins

1 t. cinnamon

½ c. applesauce

3 T. brown sugar

Bring the water to a boil and add the Cream of Wheat. Stir, then add the remaining ingredients. Remove from heat and allow to thicken slightly before serving. You can adjust the amount of cinnamon, brown sugar, and applesauce to taste.

As with the previous recipe, you don't want to overcook—otherwise, you'll end up with inedible glue. You want the cereal to be slightly runny when you take it off the heat.

Nutty Oatmeal with Raisins

(Serves four—0 mg. sodium per serving)

3 c. water

1 ½ c. quick-cooking oatmeal

¾ c. raisins

4 T. chopped walnuts

¼ c. brown sugar

1 t. cinnamon

Bring water to boil in a saucepan, then stir in the oatmeal. Keep it on the heat for about one minute, stirring rapidly, then remove. Add the remaining ingredients, then let stand for a few minutes to cool. It might look a little runny now, but as it stands, it will thicken. The trick to good oatmeal is not to add too many oats to the water. If you do, you'll end up with glue, and we all know that doesn't taste good.

Apple Raisin Oatmeal

(Serves four—0 mg. per serving)

3 c. water

1 ½ c. quick-cooking oatmeal

1 c. raisins

1 c. apple, finely chopped

¼ c. brown sugar

1 t. cinnamon

Bring water to boil in a saucepan, then stir in the oatmeal. Keep it on the heat for about one minute, stirring rapidly, then remove. Add the remaining ingredients, then let stand for a few minutes to cool. As with the previous recipe, it might look a little runny now, but don't let that fool you. It will thicken as it stands.

Walnut Breakfast Puffs

(Makes 16 puffs, depending on size—16 mg. each)

2 c. + 4 T. flour

2 t. cinnamon

2 ¼ t. sodium-free baking powder

4 T. granulated sugar

1 T. brown sugar

1 stick unsalted butter, room temperature

2 eggs

2/3 c. milk

4 T. chopped walnuts

Preheat oven to 350°. Blend the flour, cinnamon, and baking powder together, then in a separate bowl, mix the sugars with the butter and eggs until creamy. Add to the flour mixture along with the milk, and blend until well mixed. Stir in the walnuts.

Drop onto a greased or nonstick cookie sheet in mounds, then brush the tops with melted butter. Liberally sprinkle a cinnamon/sugar mixture over the top (1/4 c. sugar, 1 t. cinnamon). Bake until golden, between 12 and 15 minutes. Times will vary according to your oven, so watch the first batch. Cool on plate or wire rack.

Side Dishes

Side dishes are meant to complement the main course, but sometimes they're so tasty, they can work as the main dish themselves. The following side dishes are delicious, but make sure to cross-reference them to the sodium contents of the main dishes so you're pairing a low-sodium main dish with a higher-sodium side dish, or vice versa. And if you're ever in doubt, remember that you can never go wrong with a big green salad, loaded with vegetables.

Greek Potato Salad

(Serves four-six—155 mg. per serving, if serving four)

8 red potatoes, diced and boiled until tender

¼ c. red bell pepper, diced

1/3 c. scallions, diced

10 black olives, rinsed and sliced

1 T. red wine vinegar

2 T. water

4 T. olive oil

1 t. sugar

¾ t. dill weed

1 T. oregano

¼ c. feta cheese, crumbled

Combine the potatoes, red bell pepper, scallions, and olives in a salad bowl. In a separate bowl, mix the vinegar, water, sugar, oil, and dill to create a dressing. Toss into the potato mixture, then sprinkle the cheese over the entire dish. Refrigerate until ready to eat, ideally one hour or more.

Cream Cheese and Herb Mashed Potatoes

(Serves six—66 mg. per serving)

1 ½ lb. potatoes

4 oz. cream cheese, softened

4 T. unsalted butter

¼ c. milk

¼ t. garlic powder

1 T. dried parsley

½ t. thyme

Peel the potatoes and dice. Bring a pot of water to boil and add the potatoes, cooking until soft. Drain well, then beat with an electric mixer until smooth. You can also use a potato masher, if you don't mind the workout.

Melt the butter and stir into the potatoes, along with the softened cream cheese. Add the milk and blend, then stir in the herbs. You can adjust the milk if the potatoes are too thick or runny for your taste. If you like, you can also throw some diced scallions in there, the green parts only.

Cheese and Tomato Stuffed Potatoes
(Serves six—119 mg. per serving)

3 large baking potatoes

1 c. cheddar cheese, shredded

¼ c. green onions, diced

1 c. sour cream

¾ c. tomatoes, chopped

1/8 t. pepper (or a little more, to taste)

Bake or microwave the potatoes until tender. Cut them open lengthwise and scoop out the insides, leaving a little behind to create a strong shell with the skin. Put the potato pulp into a large bowl and mash with a fork. Stir in the cheese, onions, sour cream, tomato, and pepper, and blend until well mixed. Spoon the mixture back into the potato skins, heaping it above the rim of the skin.

For crispier potatoes, lay the filled potatoes on a baking sheet and toast in the oven until the cheese is melted.

For gooier cheese, lay the filled potatoes on a plate and microwave until the cheese is melted.

Tip: I find it easier to scoop out the potato pulp if I cradle the half potato in my palm with a hot pad between my skin and the potato. This keeps me from getting burned.

Southern California Rice

(Serves three—45 mg. per serving)

2 T. olive oil

½ c. onion, chopped

¾ c. rice

½ t. cumin

¾ t. garlic powder

1 ½ c. reduced-sodium chicken broth

½ c. no-salt-added diced tomatoes, drained

Place the oil in a skillet and heat. Add the onion and cook until clear, stirring often. Add the rice, cumin, and garlic powder. Toast the rice on all sides, stirring frequently, about 5 minutes. Add the chicken broth and diced tomatoes, then bring to a boil.

Cover, then reduce heat. Cook on low for 15 minutes, or until all the liquid is absorbed.

Corn and Barley Salad

(Serves six—5 mg. per serving)

Salad:

1 c. uncooked barley

1 (15 oz.) can corn

½ red bell pepper, diced

¼ c. green onion, sliced

Dressing:

¼ c. olive or vegetable oil

¼ c. freshly squeezed lemon juice (half of one large lemon)

2 T. cilantro leaves, torn

1/8 t. black pepper

Fill a medium saucepan half full with water and bring to a boil, then add the barley. Boil until tender, about 20 minutes.

Place corn, red pepper, and green onion in a large bowl and add drained barley. Toss to mix.

Mix all the dressing ingredients together, then toss into the salad. Serve cold or at room temperature.

Creamy Cucumber Salad

(Serves six—56 mg. per serving)

2 cucumbers, peeled and diced

2 large tomatoes, diced

½ c. sour cream

1 T. fresh dill, chopped

1 t. vinegar

½ t. sugar

Mix the cucumbers and tomatoes in a large bowl. In a separate bowl, stir the sour cream, dill, vinegar, and sugar together, then combine with the vegetables. Chill for at least an hour before serving.

Creamy Blue Cheese Dressing

(Serving size: 2 T—58 mg. per serving)

2 oz. blue cheese (you can get this crumbled in most grocery store delis)

6 oz. sour cream

4 oz. tofu

2 oz. mayonnaise

Combine all the ingredients in a blender or food processor and process until very smooth. (For a thinner dressing, use less tofu.)

This dressing is delicious—just as good as the gourmet dressings you pay a fortune for.

Ranch Dressing

(Serving size: 2 T—112 mg. per serving)

1 c. Best Foods Real Mayonnaise

1 c. buttermilk

2 t. dried minced onion

1/8 t. garlic powder

1 t. parsley flakes (increase to taste)

Put all ingredients in blender or food processor and blend for 1 minute. Refrigerate for an hour before serving.

This recipe has 150 mg. less sodium per serving than Hidden Valley Ranch dressing.

Broccoli Mango Salad

(Serves six—44 mg. per serving)

Dressing:

2 containers Yoplait Orange Crème yogurt

1 T. mayonnaise

Salad:

5 c. fresh broccoli florets, chopped and rinsed

2 mangos, peeled and diced

3 T. red onion, finely diced

Stir together the dressing ingredients, then toss together the salad ingredients until the onion is thoroughly mixed in. Add the dressing to the salad and toss. Refrigerate until ready to serve, at least 1 hour.

Spinach Berry Salad

(Serves four—45 mg. per serving)

Dressing:

¼ c. salad oil

3 T. frozen raspberry lemonade concentrate

1 T. vinegar

¼ t. Dijon mustard (or a little more, to taste)

Salad:

1 bag (6 oz.) baby spinach, washed

½ c. fresh strawberries, sliced

½ c. fresh blueberries

½ c. fresh raspberries

Blend the dressing ingredients together, and then toss the salad ingredients together. Pour the dressing over the salad and toss to coat.

Variation: You may add some red onion rings to the salad if you like.

Fruit Salad with Lemon Poppy Seed Dressing

(Serves twelve—103 mg. per serving)

Dressing:

½ c. sugar

1/3 c. freshly squeezed lemon juice

1 t. coarse ground mustard

2/3 c. salad oil

1 T. poppy seed

Salad:

10 c. Romaine lettuce, rinsed and torn into bite-sized pieces

1 c. cheddar cheese, shredded

1 c. sliced almonds

½ c. cherry-flavored dried cranberries (or regular dried cranberries, if you like)

1 medium apple, diced

1 medium pear, diced

Place the sugar, onion, lemon juice, and mustard in a blender and mix. Add the oil and blend, then add the poppy seeds.

Place all the salad ingredients in a large bowl and toss. Either add the dressing and toss to coat, or serve the dressing on the side. This is a light, flavorful, salad that you can serve to your whole family—they will really love it!

Asian Coleslaw

(Serves ten—208 mg. per serving)

1 bag (15 oz.) coleslaw mix (shredded carrots and cabbage)

½ c. creamy French dressing

¼ c. red bell pepper, chopped

¼ c. fresh cilantro leaves

½ c. unsalted peanuts

Toss all the ingredients together and serve.

Apple Slaw

(Serves ten—0 mg. per serving)

Salad:

1 bag (16 oz.) coleslaw cabbage

¼ c. green onions, sliced

2 c. Granny Smith apples, cubed

Dressing:

3 T. sugar

¼ t. apple pie spice

2 T. cider vinegar

2 T. vegetable oil

Toss all the salad ingredients together in a large bowl. Blend the dressing ingredients with a whisk until well mixed, then pour over the salad and toss to coat. Refrigerate until served.

Cucumber Orange Salad

(Serves six—45 mg. per serving)

2 cucumbers, peeled and diced

1 can (15 oz.) mandarin oranges, drained

2 T. creamy French salad dressing

¼ t. poppy seeds

Stir together all the ingredients and chill for 1 hour before serving.

Orange Ginger Green Beans

(Serves four-six—o sodium per serving)

1 lb. fresh green beans, trimmed to one-inch pieces

1 T. olive oil

1/3 c. green onions, chopped, just the green parts

1 T. gingerroot, peeled and finely chopped

½ t. orange peel, grated

Rinse the green beans, then bring them to boil in a saucepan. Cover and cook until tender, about ten minutes.

Meanwhile, heat the oil in a skillet and add the green onions and gingerroot. Sauté for 5 minutes. When the beans are done, drain them, then add the onion mixture and toss it all together with the orange peel.

Cranberry-Cherry Sauce

(Serves eight—0 mg. per serving)

1 bag (12 oz.) fresh cranberries

1/3 c. dried cherries

1 c. sugar

1 c. water

2 T. orange marmalade

In a saucepan, bring the cranberries, cherries, water, and sugar to a boil. Reduce heat to low and simmer for 10 minutes, stirring frequently, until the cranberries have all split open. Stir in the marmalade and cool for 1 hour. Refrigerate an additional hour before serving.

This is an unusual and delicious take on the old favorite. It might not be just for Thanksgiving anymore!

Mixed Fruit and Cheese Salad

(Serves six—42 mg. per serving)

1 ½ c. strawberries, sliced

2 T. blue cheese salad dressing (page 48)

1 ½ t. sugar

2 c. cantaloupe, sliced

1 c. grapes, cut in half

1 c. fresh blueberries

2 oz. mozzarella cheese, cut into small cubes

Place ¾ c. strawberries, the blue cheese dressing, and the sugar in a blender or food processor and blend well. Combine the fruit and cheese in a bowl and toss with the dressing. Serve chilled.

Main Courses

The main course is the star of your show. You might find that more attention is paid to this dish than any other. The recipes included here are divided into subheadings by the type of meat they incorporate, but there's also a vegetarian section as well. Be sure to cross-reference these meals with the side dishes you plan to serve so you're not overdoing it on the sodium.

"In every community, there is work to be done. In every nation, there are wounds to heal. In every heart, there is the power to do it."

Marianne Williamson

Turkey

Ah, turkey ... the most underappreciated of all the meats. We tend to think of turkey as being just for Thanksgiving, but it's delicious, contains less fat and sodium than chicken, and breaks up the chicken monotony. My kids always get excited when they see that I've purchased a turkey—they love the stuff and think of it as a treat.

Turkey Bowtie Salad

(Serves eight—158 mg. per serving)

1 box (12 oz.) uncooked bowtie pasta

1 lb. fresh asparagus spears, trimmed and sliced

4 c. cooked turkey, diced (baked, not lunch meat)

1 c. red bell pepper, chopped

2 t. basil

½ c. Best Foods Real Mayonnaise

2 containers Yoplait Lemon Burst yogurt

1 t. garlic powder

1 t. grated lemon peel

red leaf lettuce

Cook pasta as directed, adding the asparagus to the last five minutes of cooking time. Drain, then rinse with cold water. Drain again and allow to cool.

Place the turkey, bell pepper, and basil in a large bowl. In a smaller bowl, combine the mayonnaise, yogurt, garlic powder, and lemon peel.

Add the cooled pasta to the turkey mixture and toss, then add the dressing and toss to coat. Refrigerate until fully chilled. Serve by tossing in some chopped lettuce just before mealtime. You can stretch the servings on this dish by adding a lot of lettuce.

Glazed Turkey with Herbs

(78 mg. per 4 oz. serving)

1 large turkey, thawed, rinsed, and with neck and giblets removed

¼ c. olive oil

2 t. thyme

1 t. pepper

1 c. honey

¼ c. unsalted butter, melted

2 t. crushed dried rosemary

1 t. sage

1 t. basil

Place the turkey in an oven bag, then brush with oil. Mix the remaining ingredients in a bowl, then brush over the entire surface of the turkey. Make sure the turkey ends up on its stomach. Place the turkey in its oven bag into a roasting pan (I like getting the disposable aluminum pans) and place in the oven at 300°. Bake for around 4 hours, depending on the size of the turkey, increasing for a larger bird. The skin will turn a dark golden color, but this is normal.

Turkey Potato Chowder

(Serves six—212 mg. per serving)

1 T. unsalted butter

2 c. celery, sliced

2 T. flour

1/8 t. pepper

1 ½ c. reduced-sodium chicken broth

3 cups southern hash browns (frozen)

1 ½ c. white meat turkey, diced (roasted, not lunch meat)

1 c. frozen peas

2 c. milk

2 t. parsley flakes

1 t. dried minced onion

½ t. garlic powder

Melt the butter in a soup pot over medium heat. Add the celery and cook until tender crisp. Add the flour, pepper, and garlic powder and stir until celery is coated. Pour in the chicken broth and increase heat, stirring until the broth has come to a boil and is thickened by the flour.

Stir in the remaining ingredients and heat to boiling. Cover, reduce heat to a simmer, and cook for 10 minutes, until the potatoes are warmed through.

Chicken

All meat contains some sodium naturally. One medium-sized chicken breast contains roughly 120 mg. without adding anything else to it. The trick, then, is to combine the chicken with ingredients that don't have a lot of sodium themselves, and to not overdo the serving size. Remember that a hearty serving of salad or vegetables will go a long way toward filling you up without throwing you overboard on your sodium budget for the day.

Chicken Pasta Soup

(Serves six—370 mg. per serving)

2 boneless, skinless chicken breasts

1 pkg. (8 oz.) mushrooms

1 can (14 oz.) reduced-sodium chicken broth

1 ½ c. uncooked shell pasta

1 c. yellow summer squash, diced

½ c. red bell pepper, diced

1 ½ t. Italian seasoning

1 t. minced dried onion

Place chicken breasts in a large soup pot and cover with water. Simmer until fully cooked, then remove chicken from the pot. Reserve four cups of the cooking water and discard the rest. Dice the chicken, then return to the pot along with the four cups of reserved water, chicken broth, Italian seasoning, and onion. Bring to a boil.

Add the pasta, mushrooms, squash, and pepper and cook, covered, until the pasta is tender, about 8 minutes.

Mexican Chicken Rice Skillet

(Serves six—306 mg. per serving)

½ c. mayonnaise

1 c. reduced-sodium chicken broth

¾ c. rice, uncooked

3 T. canned green chilies, drained

½ t. cumin

1 T. chili powder

1 medium tomato, sliced

3 chicken breasts, cut in half lengthwise

In an electric skillet or large stovetop frying pan, combine the mayonnaise, broth, rice, chilies, cumin, and chili powder. Whisk together until well blended. Lay the chicken pieces on top. Bring to a boil, then cover and reduce heat. Simmer for 25 minutes, then arrange the tomatoes on top. Recover and cook for 5 more minutes. Remove from heat and let stand until all the liquid is absorbed.

You can control the heat in this dish by choosing mild green chilies and using less chili powder, if desired.

Spinach Chicken Parmesan

(Serves six—133 mg. per serving)

3 large boneless skinless chicken breasts

1/3 c. Kraft Parmesan cheese

¼ t. Italian seasoning

¼ c. green onion, diced

1 T. unsalted butter

1 T. flour

½ c. milk

5 oz. frozen spinach, thawed and drained

2 T. diced pimiento

Cut each chicken breast in half lengthwise. In a small bowl, stir together the Parmesan cheese and the Italian seasoning. Dredge both sides of each piece of chicken in the mixture and place in a baking dish. Set aside any remaining cheese mixture.

Place the butter in a small saucepan and sauté the green onions until tender crisp. Add the flour and stir vigorously until the flour has been fully incorporated into the butter. Pour in the milk and heat, stirring constantly, until the mixture is thick and bubbly. Add the drained spinach and pimiento. Spoon this evenly over the chicken pieces in the baking dish, then sprinkle the remaining cheese mixture over the top.

Bake uncovered at 350° for 30 minutes.

Tropical Chicken

(Serves six—190 mg. per serving)

4 chicken breasts

1 c. reduced-sodium chicken broth

4 T. pineapple juice concentrate, not reconstituted

1 T. honey mustard

1 clove garlic, minced

1 t. sage

1 T. honey

Preheat oven to 350°. Place chicken in a 9X13 dish and add 1 c. water, then cover with foil. Bake until the chicken is fully cooked. Meanwhile, combine the remaining ingredients in a bowl and blend well.

When the chicken is done, remove it from the pan and place it on a plate. Pour all the liquid out of the pan. Slice the chicken breast into ¼ inch slices and arrange back in the pan, then pour the broth mixture over the top. Return to the oven and simmer for an additional 10 minutes. Serve over rice, allowing the broth mixture to flavor the rice.

Cashew Chicken

(Serves six—365 mg. per serving)

2 chicken breasts, diced or cut into thin strips

2 T. Kikkoman lower-sodium soy sauce

1 T. flour

4 T. olive oil, divided in half

½ lb. mushrooms, sliced

½ onion, diced or sliced

4 c. Napa cabbage, shredded

1 t. sugar

1 t. flour

½ c. Chow Mein noodles

1 c. unsalted cashews

Place the chicken strips, soy sauce, and 1 T. flour in a bowl and mix together, then let stand at room temperature for 15 minutes, tossing frequently. Heat oil in wok or skillet and cook chicken until firm. Add onion and mushrooms, cook until tender firm, then take everything out of the wok and put into a bowl.

Put remainder of oil in wok. Stir in the cabbage and sugar, and heat from 1 to 4 minutes until the cabbage is tender crisp, not wilted. Return the chicken and vegetables to the wok. Add cashews and one additional tablespoon of soy sauce, and toss to combine. Sprinkle with a few Chow Mein noodles right before serving on a bed of rice.

Oriental Peapod and Chicken Salad

(Serves eight—153 mg. per serving)

Salad:

1 ½ c. rotini pasta

¾ lb. fresh snow peas or sugar snap peas, cut in half diagonally

1 large chicken breast, cooked and diced

1 can (8 oz.) water chestnuts, drained

1/3 c. slivered almonds

3 c. Romaine lettuce, torn into bite-sized pieces

Dressing:

½ c. mayonnaise

2 t. lower-sodium soy sauce

¼ t. pepper

¼ t. ground ginger

Cook pasta, adding the peapods in the last five minutes of cooking. Drain and rinse well with cold water. Place in a bowl and chill in refrigerator for half an hour.

Mix the chicken, onions, and water chestnuts in a large bowl. Stir in the pasta and peapods.

Stir together the dressing ingredients and toss with the salad mixture to combine. Chill for at least 3 hours. Right before serving, toss in the romaine lettuce and almonds.

Chicken Carbonara

(Serves four—283 mg. per serving)

1 T. olive oil

2 chicken breasts, cubed

½ c. evaporated milk

4 T. half and half

8 large black olives, sliced

2 T. Kraft Parmesan cheese

2 slices bacon, crisped and crumbled

Dash of pepper

Heat oil in a skillet, then add cubed chicken breasts. Brown on all sides, then add the milk and half and half. Stir until the milk begins to bubble, then add the remaining ingredients. Continue to stir until the cheese is melted. Let sit for a minute or two before serving, and the sauce will thicken. Serve over hot pasta.

Chicken in Lemon and Mushroom Sauce

(Serves four—210 mg. per serving)

2 large chicken breasts, diced

4 T. flour

2 T. olive oil

1 pkg. (8 oz.) sliced mushrooms

1 garlic clove, minced

1 c. reduced-sodium chicken broth

3 T. freshly squeezed lemon juice

1 t. fresh parsley, chopped

Take the diced chicken and coat it with flour. Heat the oil in a skillet and cook the chicken through, about 6 minutes. Test for doneness. The flour will give it a nice little breaded texture on the outside. Once the chicken is done, put into a bowl and set aside.

Put the mushrooms and garlic into the skillet and sauté until the mushrooms are tender, but not slimy. Stir in remaining ingredients and bring to a boil, adding another tablespoon of flour and stirring briskly. Let simmer about 3 minutes, then add the chicken back in. Stir to combine, and let heat another minute to blend flavors. Serve over pasta or rice.

Chicken with Creamy Chive Sauce

(Serves four—270 mg. per serving)

4 chicken breasts

1/8 t. pepper

1/8 t. salt

1 can (5 oz.) evaporated skim milk

2 t. flour

2 oz. cream cheese, softened

2 T. half and half

1 T. chives, chopped

Dash of ground nutmeg

Place the chicken breasts in a casserole dish. Put a half cup of water in the pan as well, then cover with tin foil. Bake at 350° until done, 20 minutes to half an hour, depending on your oven.

Meanwhile, put the can of milk and the flour in a saucepan and whisk thoroughly. Heat to a mild boil, whisking constantly, then add the cream cheese and the half and half. Continue whisking while the cream cheese melts, then add the chives, nutmeg, salt, and pepper.

When the chicken is done, slice it and divide onto plates, then spoon the sauce over it.

Sweet and Sour Chicken Salad

(Serves four, if a main dish, and six if a side dish. 310 mg. if divided into fourths,

and 206 mg. if divided into sixths.)

1 bag salad mix (lettuce, carrots, etc.)

1 large chicken breast, baked and diced

1 c. celery, minced

6 dried apricot halves, diced

2 T. green onions, minced

4 T. sour cream

1 T. apple cider vinegar

3 T. apricot preserves

In a large bowl, combine the chicken, salad, celery, apricots, and scallions. In a smaller bowl, stir the remaining ingredients together to form a dressing. You can either pour the dressing over the salad and toss to combine, or serve it on the side.

Chicken and Mushrooms in Parmesan Cream Sauce

(Serves four—273 mg. per serving)

2 boneless, skinless chicken breasts

4 T. all-purpose flour

1 T. each unsalted butter and olive oil

1 pkg. (8 oz.) mushrooms

½ c. milk

4   T. half and half

1   T. Parmesan cheese

1   T. parsley, chopped

Dash of pepper

Slice the chicken into strips and sauté in a skillet with the butter and olive oil. Cover and let cook until done. Remove and put on a plate. Place mushrooms in the skillet and toss until tender. Add the milk, half and half, Parmesan cheese, and parsley. Stir until cheese is melted, then add the chicken back in. Toss to coat and serve over pasta, with a sprinkle of pepper on top.

Glazed Chicken

(Serves four—307 mg. per serving)

4 t. each honey, ketchup, and reduced-sodium soy sauce

2 t. freshly squeezed lemon juice

½ t. gingerroot, peeled and grated

1 garlic clove, minced

2 chicken breasts, diced

1 T. olive oil

cooked rice or noodles

Stir together the honey, ketchup, soy sauce, lemon juice, gingerroot, and garlic. Place the chicken in a bowl, pour mixture over the top, and put in the refrigerator for half an hour.

Heat the oil in a skillet and add the chicken, sauté until chicken is cooked through, then serve with rice or noodles. The liquids combine to create a light barbecue flavor that has much less sodium than you'd get from a bottled sauce.

Creamy Cheddar Chicken
(Serves six—279 mg. per serving)

1 c. milk

1 c. reduced-sodium chicken broth

2 T. flour

4 oz. cheddar cheese, shredded

1/3 c. green onions, diced

2 chicken breasts, diced

4 T. Roma tomato, diced

cooked noodles

Whisk milk, broth, and flour together until the flour is dissolved. Place in a skillet and heat until mixture thickens, then stir in the cheese. After cheese is melted, add the chicken and scallions. Stir well. Simmer until the chicken is cooked through, then add tomato. Let simmer an additional minute, until tomato is warmed through, then serve over noodles.

Skillet Chicken and Potatoes

(Serves four—190 mg. per serving)

4 t. olive oil

5 small potatoes, scrubbed and thinly sliced

2 chicken breasts, diced

1 large carrot, diced

½ c. yellow onion, diced

½ c. red bell pepper, diced

1 small garlic clove, minced

1 can (14.5 oz) no-salt-added diced tomatoes

1 t. basil

1 t. oregano

¼ t. thyme

¼ t. pepper

Heat the oil in a skillet, then add the potatoes and the chicken. Stir until chicken is lightly browned. Remove from skillet and set aside. Put the vegetables and garlic in the skillet, adding a little more oil if needed, and sauté until tender crisp. Add the chicken and potatoes back in, add the tomatoes and the herbs, and stir well. Reduce heat to low and cover, letting simmer until potatoes are tender.

Chicken and Mushroom Filling for Quesadillas

(Makes filling for twelve quesadillas—110 mg. per quesadilla)

¼ c. unsalted butter

2 ½ t. chili powder

2 cloves garlic, minced

1 t. oregano

8 oz. mushrooms, sliced

1 chicken breast, cooked and shredded

2/3 c. onion, chopped

½ c. cilantro, chopped

1 ½ c. cheese (cheddar or Monterey Jack) shredded

Your choice of small flour or corn tortillas (be sure to take their sodium content into consideration)

Melt the butter in a large skillet. Add the chili powder, garlic, oregano, and onion and sauté for 1 minute. This smells wonderful! Add the mushrooms and toss until tender. Put the mushrooms in a large bowl, and stir in the chicken, cilantro, and cheese.

Lay the tortillas on a flat surface and put a few spoonfuls of the chicken mixture on one side of each tortilla. Fold them in half. You can now microwave them, grill them, or bake them. Absolutely delicious!

Chicken Alfredo

(Serves four—102 mg. per serving)

1 T. olive oil

2 chicken breasts, diced

½ c. tomato, chopped

1 c. mushrooms, sliced

2 garlic cloves, minced

2 T. dried basil

1 slice low-sodium bacon, crisp and crumbled

8 oz. no-salt-added tomato sauce

2 T. Kraft Parmesan cheese

4 oz. half and half

In a large skillet, heat the oil, then add the chicken. Sauté until browned, then add tomato, mushrooms, and garlic. Cook until the mushrooms are tender crisp. Add the basil, bacon, tomato sauce, and Parmesan. Heat on low for ten minutes, then add the half and half mixture, stirring well. Remove from heat and serve over hot pasta.

Spanish Chicken

(Serves four—73 mg. per serving)

4 chicken thighs (or 2 diced chicken breasts, if you prefer)

1 c. onion, chopped

8 oz. no-salt-added tomato sauce

1 t. garlic powder

1 t. paprika

1 t. basil

1 t. black pepper

1 t. parsley

¼ c. water

Put the spices in a Ziplock bag. Add the chicken and shake to coat evenly. Put the water into a large skillet and add the chicken and the onions. Cover and cook for 10 minutes, stirring occasionally. Add the tomato sauce and cook until the chicken is completely done. Serve over pasta or rice.

Pork

While some of the recipes in this book contain a crumble of bacon, you'll only find a few recipes for pork, and none for ham. Pork is high in sodium and ham is cured using salt, so unfortunately, these products will need to be used sparingly or not at all.

Dijon Pork Chops

(Serves four—333 mg. per serving)

4 pork chops

6 T. plain dried bread crumbs

2 T. Kraft Parmesan cheese

2 T. dried parsley

2 t. olive oil

1/8 t. pepper

3 t. Dijon mustard

Blend the crumbs, cheese, parsley, and pepper in a bowl until each ingredient is fully incorporated. Stir together the mustard and the oil. Place the chops first one side, then the other, into the mustard/oil mixture, then press into the crumb mixture to coat. Grill or bake 5 minutes on each side until cooked through.

Pork and Asparagus Scallopine

(Serves four—about 300 mg. per serving)

1/3 c. + 2 T. lemon herb dressing, separated

1/3 c. all-purpose flour

1 lb. boneless pork chops, about six

½ c. reduced-sodium chicken broth

1 lb. fresh asparagus spears, trimmed, cut into one-inch pieces

Place the dressing and the flour into two separate shallow bowls. Heat a nonstick skillet, then bread the pork by dredging in the dressing and then the flour. Place the pork in the skillet and cook for 2 minutes on each side or until done. Meanwhile, mix the broth and 2 T. dressing in a small bowl.

Once the pork is done, reduce heat to medium and add the broth mixture. Add the asparagus, then cover and cook until the asparagus is tender crisp, about 3 minutes. Serve with egg noodles.

Sweet and Sour Pork Chops

(Serves four—280 mg. per serving)

½ c. sweet and sour sauce

2 T. chili sauce

¼ t. ground ginger

4 boneless pork chops

½ t. garlic powder

½ t. paprika

Heat your oven to 400°. In a saucepan, mix the sweet and sour sauce, chili sauce, and the ginger. Sprinkle pork chops with garlic powder and paprika.

When the oven is hot, place the pork chops on a greased baking tray and put in the oven. Cook 8 to 10 minutes, depending on your oven, turning once. Brush the chops with the sauce a few minutes before they are completely done.

Heat remaining sauce to boiling and serve with the chops.

If you have a barbecue or a grill, this is a great barbecuing recipe. Follow the above instructions, but place the chops on the grill rather than in the oven.

Roasted Herb Pork Tenderloins

(Serves six—about 100 mg. per serving)

2 pork tenderloins

½ t. garlic pepper blend (or use equal parts garlic powder and pepper)

½ t. dried rosemary leaves, crushed

½ t. dried thyme leaves, crushed

½ t. paprika

2 t. olive oil

Preheat your oven to 425°. Blend the herbs together in a small bowl.

Brush the tenderloins with oil, then sprinkle the herbs on all sides and rub in with your fingers. Place the tenderloins in a shallow roasting pan.

Roast for 30 minutes or until done, depending on your oven. Let stand for 5 minutes before slicing.

"Fill your paper with the breathings of your heart."

William Wordsworth

Fish

Fish is considered a healthy food, but much depends on how it's prepared. Often, we go to such lengths to make fish appealing that we end up adding extra calories, cholesterol, and sodium to meet our ends. These recipes will please your crowd without the harmful additives.

Salmon with Almond Butter

(Serves four—69 mg. per serving)

4 salmon fillets, 4 oz. each (or one large salmon fillet, 16 oz.)

1 T. green onions, chopped

1/3 c. sliced almonds, unsalted

½ t. crushed basil

2 T. unsalted butter

1 T. fresh squeezed lemon juice

Preheat oven to 400°. In a saucepan or skillet, sauté the green onions in butter, then stir in the almonds, basil, and lemon juice. Spray a shallow baking dish with nonstick spray and lay the fish on it, then spread the almond mixture down the length of each piece of fish. Place in oven and bake for 8 to 10 minutes, until the fish is flaky. Be careful not to overcook.

This recipe is also delicious with halibut, coming in at 78 mg. per serving.

Parmesan Flounder Fillets

(Serves four—206 mg. per serving)

4 flounder fillets

2 T. olive oil

4 T. Kraft Parmesan cheese

Pour the oil onto a plate and roll the flounder fillets in it. Pour the Parmesan cheese onto another plate, and roll the oiled fish in the cheese. Lay the fish in a greased casserole pan and place in a preheated 350° oven. Cook until fish is flaky, about 10 minutes.

Orange Ginger Pollock
(Serves four—70 mg. per serving)

4 pollock fillets (almost any fish works well in this recipe)

¼ c. red bell pepper, diced

¼ c. green onions, diced

¼ c. carrots, diced

¼ c. red onion, diced

1 T. rice vinegar

2 T. orange juice concentrate, not reconstituted

1 t. gingerroot, grated

1 t. olive oil

2 t. Chinese sesame oil

Combine all ingredients but the fish in a mixing bowl and blend well. Using paper towels, press excess moisture out of fish, especially if the fish was frozen before use. Grease the bottom of a 9X13 pan and lay the fish inside, then top with the sauce and vegetable mixture. Place in a 350° oven and bake until the fish is flaky, about 10 minutes depending on the thickness of the filet.

Almond Salmon Sauté

(Serves four—120 mg. per serving)

Four salmon fillets, 4-6 ounces each

2 c. mushrooms, sliced

½ c. hickory-smoked almonds

2 T. olive oil

2 T. parsley, chopped

1 t. lemon juice

Heat the oven to 400°. Place the salmon on a nonstick baking dish and cook until flaky, 8 to 10 minutes. While the fish is in the oven, place the remaining ingredients in a skillet and heat through, 5 minutes. When the fish is done, lay it on a plate and top with the mushroom mixture.

Chili Lime Salmon
(Serves four—108 mg. per serving)

4 salmon fillets

2 T. butter, melted

2 T. freshly squeezed lime juice

½ t. chili powder

Mix the butter, lime juice, and chili powder together. Dredge the salmon in the butter mixture on all sides, then place in a greased baking dish. Bake at 350° for 7 to 10 minutes, until the fish is flaky.

Beef

Beef is the heartiest of all the meats. It fills us up, restores lagging strength, and just plain tastes good. These recipes will hit the spot without the additional sodium we often find in beef dishes.

Sirloin with Balsamic Glaze

(Serves four—126 mg. per serving)

16 oz. sirloin steak, sliced thin

1/3 c. balsamic vinegar

3 T. packed brown sugar

1 t. dried rosemary

2 garlic cloves, finely chopped

½ t. pepper

½ c. reduced-sodium beef broth

2   T. flour

Mix together the vinegar, sugar, rosemary, garlic, pepper, and broth. Place the meat in a glass baking dish and pour the liquid over the top. Cover and place in the refrigerator to marinate for at least 4 hours, but no more than 8 hours.

Heat a skillet and lift the meat out of the marinade. Cook on medium heat until done, just a few minutes on each side. Place the remaining marinade in a saucepan and bring to a boil, then add the flour, whisking vigorously to create gravy to serve over the cooked meat.

Note: you can also use thicker cuts of meat and cook on your outdoor grill.

Pepper Beef Stroganoff

(Serves four—153 mg. per serving)

1 T. unsalted butter

½ lb. sirloin steak, diced or cut into thin strips

¼ t. black pepper

¼ t. garlic powder

1 ½ c. fresh mushrooms, sliced

¼ c. reduced-sodium beef broth

1 t. chili sauce

¼ c. French onion dip

Wide noodles

Melt butter in a skillet and add beef strips. Sprinkle with garlic powder and pepper. Toss to coat, then cook until done, 5 to 8 minutes. Add the mushrooms and sauté for 1 minute, then add the broth and chili sauce. Simmer for 3 minutes, then reduce heat. Stir in the French onion dip until well blended, then serve over hot noodles.

Bavarian Beef Roast

(Serves eight—310 mg. per serving)

1 3 lb. rump roast

3 T. coarse-ground mustard

1 T. creamy horseradish sauce

1 envelope brown gravy mix

½ c. apple juice

½ c. water

3 T. flour

1 T. green onions, chopped

Place roast in crock pot. Mix the mustard, horseradish sauce, and dry gravy mix together in a small bowl, then spread the mixture on the sides and top of the roast. Pour the apple juice around the sides of the roast, being careful not to wash off the sauce.

Cook on low setting for 9 hours. Remove roast from crock pot and pour juices into a sauce pan. Heat the juices to boiling. In a separate bowl, whisk the water and flour together to form a paste, then add to the boiling juices to thicken. Whisk constantly until well blended and thickened into gravy. Add the green onions and serve over the roast.

Steak and Peppers

(Serves four—80 mg. per serving)

16 oz. beef tenderloin steak, cut into thin strips

½ t. olive oil

1/8 t. black pepper

1/8 t. garlic powder

¼ onion, diced

½ red bell pepper and ½ yellow bell pepper, cut into thin strips

1 clove garlic, minced

1/8 t. paprika

1/3 c. water

1/3 c. evaporated milk

1 T. flour

Heat the oil in a skillet, and add the sliced meat. Toss with black pepper and garlic powder and sauté until cooked through. Remove from heat and slide meat onto a plate. Pour the juices into a dish to be used later.

Put the garlic in the skillet and sauté until golden, then add the peppers and onions. Cook until tender, about 5 minutes. Slide onto a plate and set aside.

Place the milk, water, reserved meat juice, and paprika in the skillet and bring to a boil. Whisk in the flour and stir until thickened. Add back in the meat and the peppers and simmer until just warmed through. Serve over noodles or rice.

Chili Con Carne with Beans

(Serves eight—122 mg. per serving)

2 1b. ground beef

3 T. olive oil

1 medium onion, chopped

1 c. red bell peppers, chopped

½ t. garlic, minced

½ t. pepper

1 t. cumin

1 t. cayenne

1 T. chili powder

3 c. water

8 oz. no-salt-added tomato paste

4 c. no-salt-added tomatoes, diced

4 c. no-salt-added kidney beans

Place the ground beef in your largest soup kettle or skillet. Brown, then drain off the fat and set aside. Heat the oil in the kettle or skillet, adding the onions and then the red pepper and garlic. Sauté until tender. Add the pepper, cumin, cayenne, and chili powder. Stir continually until the spices begin to brown.

If you're using a skillet, transfer mixture to your large soup pot. Add water, tomato paste, and the canned tomatoes with their juice. Add the kidney beans and the beef. Bring to a simmering boil, then reduce heat and cover. Simmer for 3 hours on low to allow the flavors to blend. Stir every 15 minutes.

Hamburger Stroganoff

(Serves four—107 mg. per serving)

1 lb. ground beef

1 onion, chopped

4 oz. mushrooms, sliced

1 T. flour

½ c. reduced-sodium beef broth

2 T. no-salt-added tomato paste

1 c. sour cream

Using a large skillet, brown the ground beef with the mushrooms and onion. Drain, then sprinkle flour over the top and stir to mix in. Add broth and cook until thickened, stirring constantly. Remove from heat and stir in sour cream. Serve over hot noodles or rice.

Beef Alfredo with Pasta

(Serves five—300 mg. per serving)

2 ¼ c. penne pasta

1 lb. lean ground beef

3 T. green onions, diced

10 oz. prepared Alfredo sauce (I prefer Ragu)

4 Roma tomatoes, diced

1 t. dried basil

While the pasta is cooking, brown the ground beef and drain. Blot off excess grease with a paper towel. Add the onions and Alfredo sauce, and heat until bubbly. Stir in the drained pasta, tomatoes, and basil, and heat through. Add pepper to taste, if desired.

Pizza

(Sodium content will vary)

Crust: *(0 mg)*

1 2/3 c. warm water

2 T. olive oil

3 T. sugar

5 c. flour

1 t. yeast

Place the warm water, oil and sugar in a large bowl, then sprinkle the yeast over the top. Allow to sit for 5 minutes. Then stir in the flour a little at a time, kneading it with your hands as the dough becomes thicker. When all the flour is incorporated and the dough is smooth, cover with plastic wrap and allow to sit in the refrigerator for 15 minutes.

Remove the dough from the fridge and punch it down, then press it out on a greased cookie sheet. This recipe will make enough dough for two pizzas.

Sauce: *(25 mg. per slice)*

Use the marinara sauce recipe on page 111.

Toppings:

Mozzarella cheese, 175 mg. per oz.

Cheddar cheese, about 170 mg. per oz.

Red and green bell peppers, 0 mg.

Diced tomatoes, fresh, 0 mg.

Diced onions, fresh, 0 mg.

Mushrooms,   0 mg.

Pineapple, 0 mg.

Zucchini, 0 mg.

Spinach, 0 mg.

Ground beef, 85 mg. per 4 oz., cooked

You can get creative and add just about anything to your pizza. I do encourage you to avoid olives, artichokes, pepperoni, sausage, and Canadian bacon, as those all contain a high level of sodium. Substitute browned ground beef for the other meats.

Taco Seasoning

(0 mg.)

1 T. chili powder

¼ t. garlic powder

¼ t. onion powder

¼ t. crushed red pepper flakes

¼ t. oregano

½ t. paprika

1 ½ t. cumin

1 t. pepper

Blend these spices together and then add to your ground beef to create the perfect filling for tacos, burritos, and taco salads. This easy mix will save you over 400 mg. per serving compared to the taco seasoning you purchase at the store.

Vegetarian

Dinner doesn't always have to include meat. In fact, the more vegetarian dishes you incorporate into your diet, the better for your overall heart health. Meat contains sodium and cholesterol, so while you should eat enough to sustain your protein, you should try to cut back on it a little bit for optimum health results.

Vegetarian Lasagna

(Serves twelve—150 mg. per serving)

Sauce:

Use the marinara sauce recipe on page 111.

Other Ingredients:

1 t. olive oil

2 cups zucchini, diced and rinsed

1 egg

2 c. ricotta cheese (don't substitute cottage cheese!)

1 T. dried basil

1/8 t. pepper

9 lasagna noodles, cooked

1 10 oz. package frozen spinach, thawed and squeezed dry

¼ c. Kraft Parmesan cheese

2 c. mozzarella cheese, shredded

Preheat your oven to 350˚ and lightly grease a 9X13 pan, or use a nonstick spray.

Sauté the zucchini in the olive oil until tender crisp, then remove from heat. In a medium-sized bowl, mix together the ricotta, basil, egg, and pepper. Stir until thoroughly combined.

Put three lasagna noodles side by side in the bottom of the baking dish. Top with ½ c. marinara sauce, spread evenly. Then place ½ of the ricotta mixture on top of that, also spreading evenly. Using two forks, pull apart the pieces of spinach and sprinkle ½ of it over the ricotta, then top with ½ the cooked zucchini. Sprinkle lightly with Parmesan cheese, then cover with one handful of mozzarella cheese.

Layer on three more noodles, and repeat with another half cup of sauce, the remaining ricotta, the rest of the spinach, and the rest of the zucchini. Sprinkle with Parmesan and cover with another handful of mozzarella cheese.

Lay the remaining three noodles on top and cover with another ½ c. of sauce. Sprinkle a little mozzarella on top as a garnish.

Cover with tin foil and bake at 350° for 30 minutes, then uncover and bake for another 10. Allow to sit on the counter to cool for 10 minutes before cutting.

Alternatives: Use mushrooms in place of the zucchini, or in place of the spinach. You can also add ½ c. diced onion to the zucchini and sauté them together.

Southwestern Black Bean Salad

(Serves six—220 mg. per serving)

1 can (15.5 oz.) black beans, reduced sodium, drained and rinsed

1 can (15.5 oz.) corn, reduced sodium, drained and rinsed

6 Roma tomatoes, diced

2 oz. cheddar cheese, shredded

3 T. sour cream

2 t. each red wine vinegar, chopped fresh cilantro, and olive oil

1 bag mixed salad greens

In a large salad bowl, mix together the beans, corn, and tomatoes. Toss in the cheese, then stir in the sour cream.

In a small bowl, stir the vinegar, cilantro, and olive oil together, then combine with the rest. Put the mixture in the fridge for at least an hour before serving.

When it's time to eat, place a handful of salad lettuce in the center of each plate and top with the corn and bean mixture. You could put a few tortilla chips on the side, if you don't go overboard.

Pasta with Broccoli

(Serves four—155 mg.per serving)

3 t. olive oil

2 large garlic cloves, diced

4 c. broccoli crowns, chopped

½ c. no-salt-added canned tomatoes, diced

1 t. oregano

½ c. lower-sodium chicken broth

4 T. Kraft Parmesan cheese

cooked pasta

Heat the oil in a skillet and sauté the garlic until golden. Add the broccoli and toss until tender crisp, then add the tomatoes, oregano, and chicken broth. Simmer for two minutes, then add the cheese. Stir well, then serve over the pasta. A light, delicious meal that won't hurt your cholesterol, either!

Cheesy Tortellini Salad

(Serves eight—300 mg. per serving)

1 9 oz. package refrigerated or frozen three-cheese tortellini

4 c. broccoli crowns, chopped

½ c. Italian vinaigrette dressing

1 t. basil

3 cups tomato, diced

1 c. cheddar cheese, shredded

Cook the tortellini according to package directions and drain. Boil or steam the broccoli until tender crisp—you don't want it mushy. Toss together and add the tomato, basil, and dressing, then place in the refrigerator for an hour.

Remove and add the cheese, tossing again. When the salad is completely chilled, serve.

You can use this as a main dish or a side. You can also create your own dressing with ½ c. olive oil, 1 T. red wine vinegar, and Italian seasonings to taste, and cut back some of the sodium content further. If you choose to go with the bottled variety, be sure to read labels and get the brand with the least sodium.

Marinara Sauce

(95 mg. per ¼ c. serving)

1 can (14.5 oz.) crushed tomatoes in puree

1 t. Italian seasoning

½ t. garlic powder

Place all ingredients in a saucepan and simmer for 10 minutes. You can adjust the seasoning and garlic powder to suit your own tastes. This recipe will save you 400 mg. of sodium over purchased sauce.

Cheesy Vegetable Chowder

(Serves six—340 mg. per serving)

2 c. potatoes, diced

1 c. carrots, diced

1 c. celery, diced

½ onion, diced

¼ c. unsalted butter

¼ c. flour

2 c. milk

½ c. Kraft Parmesan cheese

1 can (15 oz.)creamed corn

Place the potatoes, carrots, celery, and onion in a soup pot and cover with water. Bring to a boil and simmer until all the vegetables are soft, around 15 minutes. Take off the heat and let cool for 10 minutes. Put the vegetables and the water into a blender or food processor, and blend until smooth.

Place the butter and flour in a saucepan and bring to a boil, stirring constantly. Add the flour, whisking briskly, then add the cheese. As soon as all the ingredients are incorporated, remove from heat.

Return the vegetables to the pot and stir in the milk mixture. Add the corn and reheat before serving.

Bean and Barley Soup

(Serves eight—252 mg. per serving)

2 t. olive oil

2 ½ c. baby carrots, thinly sliced

2 ½ c. celery, thinly sliced

½ c. onion, finely chopped

½ c. quick-cooking barley

1 can (15 oz.) Great Northern beans, drained and rinsed

1 can (14.5 oz.) can no-salt-added diced tomatoes

1 can (8 oz.) tomato sauce, no salt added

1 t. oregano

1 t. basil

1 t. garlic powder

3 c. water

In a soup pot, heat the oil, then add the carrots, celery, and onion. Cook for 3 minutes, stirring constantly.

Put all the remaining ingredients into the pot and bring to a simmer. Cook for 15 to 20 minutes, until the barley is cooked through.

"If you really want to make a friend, go to someone's house and eat with him...The people who give you their food give you their heart."

Cesar Chavez

Cookies and Desserts

Desserts aren't salty—they're sweet, so we often don't think about their sodium content. Surprise—they can contain as much sodium as a salty snack. These recipes will satisfy that craving without sending your blood pressure into a tailspin.

Note: baked goods created with unsalted butter will have a slightly different texture than what you're perhaps used to, but they are still delicious!

M & M Cookies

(Makes 24—7 mg. each)

1 c. unsalted butter

¾ c. white sugar

¾ c. brown sugar

2 ½ c. flour

½ tsp. sodium-free baking powder

2 eggs

½ t. vanilla

1 ½ c. M & M candies, divided

Preheat oven to 350°. Blend the butter, sugars, eggs, and vanilla together, then beat in the flour and baking powder. Coarsely chop 1 c. M & M candies and blend them into the batter. Drop onto cookie sheets by rounded spoonfuls, then press M & Ms into the tops of the cookies. Bake 10 to 12 minutes, depending on your oven.

Sugar Cookies

(Makes sixty—0 mg. each)

2 ½ c. flour

2 t. Cream of Tartar

2 t. sodium-free baking soda

1 c. unsalted butter

1 t. vanilla

1 c. sugar

½ c. egg substitute or 2 large eggs

Stir together the dry ingredients. Cream the butter, vanilla and sugar until light, then add the eggs and beat well. Blend in the dry ingredients, mixing well, then chill 1 hour.

Shape dough into 1-inch balls and place 2 ½ inches apart on a greased cookie sheet. Sprinkle with colored sugar if desired. Bake at 375° for 8 minutes or until golden. Remove to racks to cool.

The only sodium in this recipe will come from the frosting you choose. The good news is, most frostings don't contain a lot of sodium, so you can enjoy without the guilt.

Pumpkin Chocolate Chip Cookies
(Makes thirty—8 mg.each)

1 c. (2 sticks) unsalted butter, softened

1 c. white sugar

1 c. brown sugar

2 large eggs

1 t. vanilla

1 c. canned pumpkin

3 c. flour

2 ½ t. sodium-free baking powder

1 t. cinnamon

½ t. ginger

¼ t. nutmeg

2 c. (12 oz. bag) milk or semi-sweet chocolate chips

Cream together the butter and sugars, then blend in eggs, vanilla, and pumpkin. Add the dry ingredients and mix until creamy, and then add in the chocolate chips. Bake at 350° for 15-20 minutes, depending on your oven. Remove from oven and let cool on the rack. You honestly will not miss the salt in these fluffy, delicious cookies.

White Chocolate/Cranberry Cookies

(Makes thirty-six—10 mg. each)

½ c. shortening

1 c. brown sugar

1 large egg

1 t. vanilla

1 ¾ c. flour

1 t. sodium-free baking soda

¼ c. buttermilk

½ c. white chocolate chips

½ c. dried cranberries

Beat shortening and sugar together until fluffy. Add the egg and vanilla. Mix the dry ingredients together, then add to the sugar mixture, along with the buttermilk. Beat until smooth, then stir in the chocolate chips and cranberries. Drop about 2 inches apart on a greased cookie sheet. Bake at 375° for 8 to 10 minutes until lightly browned.

Chocolate Chip Cookies

(Makes forty-eight—3 mg. each)

Cream together:

1 c. packed brown sugar

1 c. white sugar

1 c. unsalted butter

2 eggs

2 t. vanilla

Blend with mixer until light and fluffy, then add:

3 c. flour

½ t. sodium-free baking powder

Mix well, then stir in chocolate chips. Bake on heavy duty cookie sheets at 325° degrees for 12-15 minutes. Pull out when just barely done and let finish cooking on the sheet. Do not overbake.

Orange Chocolate Chip Cookies

(Makes forty-eight—3 mg. each)

Cream together:

1 c. packed brown sugar

1 c. white sugar

1 c. unsalted butter

2 eggs

2 t. vanilla

1 t. grated orange zest

1 T. freshly squeezed orange juice

Blend with mixer until light and fluffy, then add:

3 c. flour

½ t. sodium-free baking powder

Mix well, then stir in one bag semi-sweet chocolate chips. Bake on heavy duty cookie sheets at 325° for 12-15 minutes. Pull out when just barely done and let finish cooking on the sheet. Do not overbake.

This recipe takes the standard chocolate chip cookie recipe on the previous page and gives it a whole new twist with the orange.

Carrot Cake

(Serves fifteen—49 mg. per serving)

Cake:

2 c. sugar

1 ½ c. oil

4 eggs

1 c. flour

1 c. whole wheat flour

2 tsp. sodium-free baking powder

1 T. cinnamon

2 t. vanilla

3 c. carrots, grated

4 oz. pecans, chopped

1 c. raisins

½ c. crushed pineapple, with juice

1 c. coconut

Frosting:

¼ c. unsalted butter, softened

4 oz. cream cheese, softened

½ 1b. powdered sugar

1 t. vanilla

Combine the sugar and oil in a large bowl, and stir. Add eggs and vanilla, and mix again. Add the flour, baking powder, and cinnamon, then beat with a hand mixer. Stir in the carrots, nuts, raisins, pineapple, and coconut by hand. Pour into a greased 9X13 cake pan and bake at 325° for 45 minutes.

To make the frosting, beat the butter and cream cheese together, then add the sugar and vanilla, blending until thick and creamy. Spread over the fully cooled cake and enjoy.

Note: when powdered sugar is opened, it tends to take on the flavor of the items next to it in the cupboard. It's best to use a fresh bag of powdered sugar when making frosting.

Caramel Pecan Brownies

(Serves nine—47 mg. per serving)

12 caramels, unwrapped

1/3 c. unsalted butter

2 T. milk

¾ c. sugar

2 eggs

½ t. vanilla

¾ c. flour

½ t. sodium-free baking powder

½ c. chopped pecans

Combine the caramels, butter, and milk in a saucepan over low heat. Stir frequently until the caramels begin to melt, then stir constantly to incorporate the butter and milk into the caramels. After the mixture is fully incorporated, remove from heat and stir in the sugar. Add the eggs and vanilla, stir well, and set aside.

Combine the flour and baking powder in a mixing bowl, then add the caramel mixture. Stir well, then add the pecans, stirring again. Pour into a greased 9X9 baking dish and bake at 350° for 20 minutes, or until an inserted knife comes out clean.

Texas Sheetcake-style Brownies

(Serves twenty—13 mg. per serving)

Brownies:

1 c. unsalted butter

1/3 c. baking cocoa

2 c. granulated sugar

4 eggs

1 ¾ c. flour

2 t. vanilla

Frosting:

1/3 c. unsalted butter

5 T. baking cocoa

3 T. milk

2 c. powered sugar

1 t. vanilla

To make the brownies, melt the butter in a saucepan, then pour into a large mixing bowl. Add the vanilla, sugar, and cocoa, and beat at medium speed. Add the eggs and mix again, then add the flour. Blend well. Pour into a greased 9X13 pan and bake at 350° for 30 minutes. Test by inserting a knife into the center. When the knife comes out clean, remove brownies from oven. Cool completely, then frost.

To make the frosting, melt the butter in a saucepan, then pour into a small mixing bowl. Add the cocoa and milk, then slowly blend in the sugar. Adjust the consistency of the frosting by adding more sugar for a thicker frosting and more milk for a thinner frosting.

Note: when powdered sugar is opened, it tends to take on the flavor of the items next to it in the cupboard. It's best to use a fresh bag of powdered sugar when making frosting.

Mississippi Mud Cake

(Serves fifteen—36 mg. per serving)

1 c. unsalted butter

2 c. sugar

4 eggs

1 ½ c. flour

4 T. unsweetened baking cocoa

2 c. miniature marshmallows

15 t. chocolate syrup

Soften the butter in the microwave. In a mixing bowl, cream together the eggs and sugar, then add the flour, cocoa, and softened butter. Blend well. Put mixture in a greased 9X13 pan and bake at 350° for 30 minutes. Check for doneness by inserting a knife until it comes out clean. When done, remove from the oven and sprinkle the marshmallows evenly across the top. Return to the oven just until the marshmallows have melted. Allow to cool completely.

To serve, place piece on a dish and then drizzle with one teaspoon of chocolate syrup.

Blueberry Swirl Pie

(Serves eight—44 mg. per serving)

Filling:

1 box Jell-O sugar-free lemon gelatin

½ c. boiling water

1 can (21 oz.) blueberry pie filling

¼ c. sour cream

Crust:

½ c. unsalted butter

¾ c. flour

½ c. quick cooking oats

½ c. chopped pecans (or walnuts)

2 T. sugar

Dissolve gelatin in boiling water. Stir in the pie filling and mix until completely incorporated, then place in the fridge to set, about 1 hour.

Meanwhile, microwave the butter until melted, then stir in the flour, oats, nuts, and sugar. Press mixture onto the bottom and sides of a buttered pie plate to form an even crust. Bake at 400° for 10 minutes, until the edges are golden. Allow to cool completely.

Once the pie filling has set, spread it in the pie crust. Place dollops of sour cream here and there all over the top, and then swirl it in to the top layer of filling. Refrigerate for another hour before serving.

"Without a rich heart, wealth is an ugly beggar."

Ralph Waldo Emerson

Appendix

Seven-day Sample Meal Plan

By combining higher sodium meals with lower sodium meals, you can achieve proper balance throughout the day. The following menu is an example of how this can be done—of course, you're under no obligation to combine the recipes exactly this way.

Monday
Breakfast: Fruit Salad (page 29) - 24 mg.
    Banana Pecan Cream of Wheat (page 38) – 56 mg.
Lunch: Cheese and Tomato Stuffed Potatoes (page 46) – 119 mg.
    Baby carrots
Snack: Two Pumpkin Chocolate Chip Cookies (page 122) -16 mg.
Dinner: Steak and Peppers (page 101) – 80 mg.
    Greek Potato Salad (page 44) –154 mg.
    Total Sodium Consumption: 449 mg.

Tuesday
Breakfast: 2 Pancakes (page 31) – 84 mg.
    Pancake Syrup (page 30) – 0 mg.
    Scrambled Egg –56 mg.
Lunch: Fruit Salad w/Lemon Poppy Seed Dressing (page 54) – 103 mg.
Snack: 2 M&M Cookies (page 120) – 14 mg.
Dinner: Mexican Chicken Rice Skillet (page 69) – 306 mg.
    Green Salad with Blue Cheese Dressing (page 50) - 58 mg.
    Total Sodium Consumption: 612 mg.

Wednesday
Breakfast: Veggie Breakfast Bake (page 37) – 256 mg.
Lunch: Creamy Cucumber Salad (page 49) -56 mg.
    Southern California Rice (page 47) - 45 mg.
Snack: Apple Slaw (page 56) – 0 mg.
Dinner: Broccoli Mango Salad (page 52) – 44 mg.
    Sirloin with Balsamic Glaze (page 98) – 126 mg.
Dessert: Brownies (page 129) – 13 mg.
    Total Sodium Consumption: 540 mg.

Thursday
Breakfast: Nutty Oatmeal with Raisins (page 40) – 0 mg.
Snack: Banana, slice of cheese – 174 mg.

Lunch: Pepper Beef Stroganoff (page 99) - 153 mg.

                Orange Ginger Green Beans (page 58) – 0 mg.

Dinner: Salmon with Almond Butter (page 92) – 69 mg.

                Cream Cheese and Herb Mashed Potatoes (page 45) – 66 mg.

                Cucumber Orange Salad (page 57) – 45 mg.

Total Sodium Consumption: 507 mg.

Friday

Breakfast: Crab Quiche (page 36)- 213 mg.

Snack: Apple

Lunch: Oriental Peapod and Chicken Salad (page 73) – 153 mg.

Dinner: Bavarian Beef Roast (page 100) – 310 mg.

                Green Salad with Ranch Dressing (page 51) – 112 mg.

Total Sodium Consumption: 788 mg.

Saturday

Breakfast: Cranberry Sauce Muffins (page 32) – 12 mg.

Snack: String cheese, pear - 210 mg.

Lunch: Beef Alfredo with Pasta (page 105) – 300 mg.

Dinner: Cashew Chicken (page 72) - 365 mg.

Total Sodium Consumption: 887 mg.

Sunday

Breakfast: Cinnamon Applesauce Cream of Wheat (page 39) – 56 mg.

                Scrambled egg – 56 mg.

Snack: Almond Poppy Seed Bread (page 35) – 18 mg.

                Slice of cheese – 174 mg.

Lunch: Chili con Carne with Beans (page 102) – 122 mg.

Dinner: Spinach Chicken Parmesan (page 70) – 133 mg.

                Green salad

Total Sodium Consumption: 559 mg.

Low-sodium Choices at Fast Food Restaurants

It's ideal to avoid eating at fast food restaurants if at all possible, but there are times when we don't have much choice. I visited the Web sites of seven popular fast food establishments to learn which menu items contain the least amount of sodium per serving, not including the dessert items. Hard to believe, but at most restaurants, you'll want to stay away from the salads.

Arby's:

Jr. Roast Beef Sandwich	740 mg.
Small Curly Fries	791 mg.
Regular Onion Petals	249 mg.

Burger King:

4 pc. Chicken Tenders	490 mg.
Whopper Jr. (no mayo)	500 mg.
Small Onion Rings	490 mg.
Small Fries	590 mg.

Carl's Jr.:

Charbroiled Chicken Salad, no dressing	710 mg.
Chili Cheese Burger	960 mg.
Kids' Fries	960 mg.
Onion Rings	550 mg.

McDonald's:

Small Hamburger	530 mg.
Small French Fries	140 mg.

Subway:

Veggie Delite	500 mg.
Roast Beef Mini Sub	690 mg.

Taco Bell:

Regular Taco	380 mg.
Nachos (chips and cheese only)	530 mg.

Wendy's:

Jr. Hamburger	490 mg.
Small French Fry	290 mg.
Side Salad	380 mg.

Recommended Reading:

Baron-Faust, Rita, *Preventing Heart Disease: What Every Woman Should Know* (New York: Hearst Books, 1995)

Kra, Seigfried J. *What Every Woman Must Know about Heart Disease* (New York: Warner Books, 1996)

Sheps, Sheldon G. *Mayo Clinic on High Blood Pressure* (Rochester: Mayo Clinic, 2002)

Helpful Web Sites:

http://www.medicinenet.com/high_blood_pressure/page3.htm

http://www.saltinstitute.org/28.html

http://www.cdc.gov/DHDSP/library/fs_men_heart.htm

About the Author

Tristi Pinkston is the author of eight, the mother of four, the wife of one, a homeschooler, a Cubmaster, a mentor, a freelance editor, an online writing instructor, a trier-of-all-things new, and a slayer of dragons. When she's not looking for her next challenge to overcome, she's watching a good movie, taking a nap, or obsessively checking her e-mail.

www.tristipinkston.com

www.tristipinkston.blogspot.com

www.tristipinkstonediting.blogspot.com

Made in the USA
San Bernardino, CA
01 February 2015